This Book is a Gift

| To |
| From |
| On the Occasion of |
| Date |

Become The Best! Release

Understanding How You Can Give Your Best To Your World

SUNDAY A. EZEKIEL

Become The Best! Release Your Potential
Copyright © 2014 by:
Sunday A. Ezekiel

Repackaged, edited and reprinted in 2017
ISBN: 978-198-6637-213

Published in Nigeria by:
DW-Impact Ltd, Lagos – Nigeria
All rights reserved. No portion of this publication may be reproduced, stored in retrieval system, or transmitted in any form by any means – electronic, mechanical, photocopying, recording, or any other – without the prior written permission of the publisher, except for brief quotations in printed reviews, magazines, articles etc.
For further enquiries, distribution or permission, contact:
Dreamers World Christian Centre
Phone:
+234-8035122385, +234-7082982341
Email:
info@dreamersworldng.org
Website:
www.dreamersworldng.org
Facebook Pages:

Become The Best! Release Your Potential

Contents

Introduction

Chapter 1   Understanding Potential   01

Chapter 2   Discovering Your Potential   09

Chapter 3   The Purpose of Potential   21

Chapter 4   Releasing Your Potential   35

Chapter 5   Maximizing Your Potential   49

Introduction

What lies behind us and what lies before us are tiny matters compared to what lies within us.
Ralph Waldo Emerson

It is only what is discovered that can be recovered. That is why undiscovered and unreleased potential results in unaccomplished destiny.

Man is a wonder by virtue of creation. This is because God created man in His image and likeness with all the ability in Him released into man. In other words, everything in God is in man. All the virtues that are inherent in God, The manufacturer are inherent in man His product. This truth becomes our focus of discussion all over this book.

The nature of the source from which a product was made determines the component of the product. And since man is a product of God, then he possesses the same component as God, his Source.
It is imperative to know that your attitude is largely a product of your self-concept – the picture you have of yourself. The issue of self-concept and self-image must first be establish in our minds before we can really understand the potential inherent in us and release them to fulfill our destiny.

God created man in His image; therefore, man is expected to have a concept of himself in line with who God is.

In this book, you will gain a full understanding of the great deposit that is loaded into you at creation. Also, you will come to the knowledge of the fact that what you are loaded with in form of potential is given you for the purpose of fulfilling your destiny and become a blessing to the world.

I am sure that by the time you are through reading

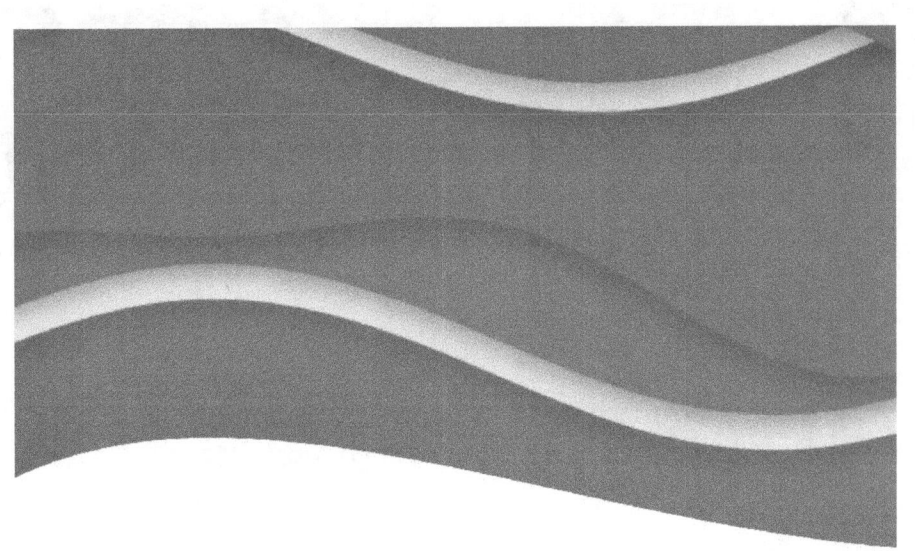

CHAPTER ONE

UNDERSTANDING POTENTIAL

CHAPTER
UNDERSTANDING POTENTIAL

A wise man will hear, and will increase learning; and a man of understanding shall attain unto wise counsels.

Understanding is the key to deriving maximum benefits from every subject of life. In other words, man will only experience the blessing of the issues he has understanding of. And that understanding will only come by gaining insight into the nitty-gritty of such issues.

Also, our reactions towards life's matters are determined by our level of understanding of the matters. That is why it is important to keep learning until one gain the full understanding of every issue that pertains to ones fulfillment of in life.

The subject of potential is of utmost important in determining the fulfillment or otherwise of man's destiny. I am of the opinion that until potential is understood, discovered and released, fulfillment of destiny is not in view for any man.

If you desire to become a person of impact and exploits by leaving an indelible mark on your generation, you must have a very good understanding of potential. The reason is that until you understanding what it means, you may not discover yours. And if you do not discover your potential, you will not release it in order to enhance the full delivery of your mandate on earth.

In this chapter, I will be showing you what potential means and you will gain the knowledge that you have within you all the potential you need to fulfill your destiny in life.

What is Potential?

Potential is that divine ability yet to be used, but crying out for expression. It is that divine energy in man that is still dormant. Potential is that inner power that is yet to be tapped. It is that divine endowment that is still hidden. Also, potential is that greatness that is yet to manifest. It is the latent (dormant) qualities or abilities that may be developed for future success, but yet to be.

To be more specific, potential is God's ability, power, endowment or energy that is capable of bringing man to the fulfillment of the purpose for which God created him.

The encyclopedia defines potential as:
- *Inherent ability or capacity for growth, development, or coming into being.*
- *Something possessing the capacity for growth or development.*
- *Capable of being but not yet in existence; latent.*
- *Having possibility, capability, or power.*

Also, Dr. Myles Munroe defines potential as unexposed ability, reserved power, untapped strength, capped capabilities, unused success, dormant gifts, hidden talents and latent power.

He said, further, "potential is what you can do that you haven't done; where you can go that you haven't gone; who you can be that you are yet to be; how far you can reach that you haven't yet reached; what you can see that you haven't yet seen; what you can accomplish that you haven't yet accomplished."

To put it in a different way, it does not matter what you have done before now, there are still things that you can do that is hidden in you. You need to understand that the fulfillment of your destiny is related to your potential. If you can dream of doing anything, that is the evidence that you can do it. The dream in your heart now, no matter how impossible it may appear, it can become a reality because in as much as you can dream it you have within you the potential to fulfill it.

Potential is the sum total of who you are that you are yet to reveal. Your potential is what God deposited in you that can change your world.

Just as you cannot separate a man from a woman to have a baby, you cannot separate your potential from the fulfillment of your destiny. In other words potential and fulfillment of destiny are inseparable.

Every living thing that God created was blessed with potential. Your potential comes from God who is the Source from where you came. And He has planted within you the ability to be much more than you are at any moment.

You are a living wonder on earth. When God created you, he released Himself into you because He spoke to Himself and you came forth. That means your potential is defined by God's potential. In other words, what is in God in the form of potential is what is in you as your potential. God, who is your Source, is the only one who determines what you can do on earth. Therefore, the quality of your potential is determined by God's potential. God, your Source, created you in His image so that you can share His potential. (Genesis 1:26-28)

The vision of what can happen through you cannot be separated from the ability of God in you in the form of gifts and talents. What you can do springs from the knowledge of the resources that you have to do it. Everyman on earth is endowed by God with resources according to each one's ability which is defined by God's ability.

> Matthew 25:14-15
> *For the kingdom of heaven is as a man travelling into a far country, who called his own servants, and delivered unto them his goods.*
> *And unto one he gave five talents, to another two, and to another one;* **to every man according to his several ability;** *and straightway took his journey.*

That explains the fact that every creature of God made in His image is divinely endowed according to what each one has capacity to handle as determined by God's capacity.

You are supposed to operate naturally like God, your Source. In other words, you natural mode of operation is the same as God's because, you came out of Him when He spoke to Himself. And off cause, the product always has the nature of its source. You are expected to think, talk and act like God because you have everything He has in Him by virtue of creation.

Understanding Potential

Nobody knows who you are except God who has blessed you with potential. The ability is in you, but your understanding, discovery and release of it is the key to your fulfillment. There is no one who is not gifted by God one way or the other.

It is important to understand that you have within you all the qualities and elements that are necessary to make you a success. Your major task is the discovery and development of that gift that God has already given you.

Please, understand that, you are not disadvantaged. You have been given all you need to become the success God made you to be. You only need to accept responsibility for the release of that potential that is in you.

However, your success in life in the pursuit of your dream is not determined by the potential alone, but by what you do with that potential. In other words, it is not whether you have the ability or not; rather, it is whether you put what you have to use that matters.

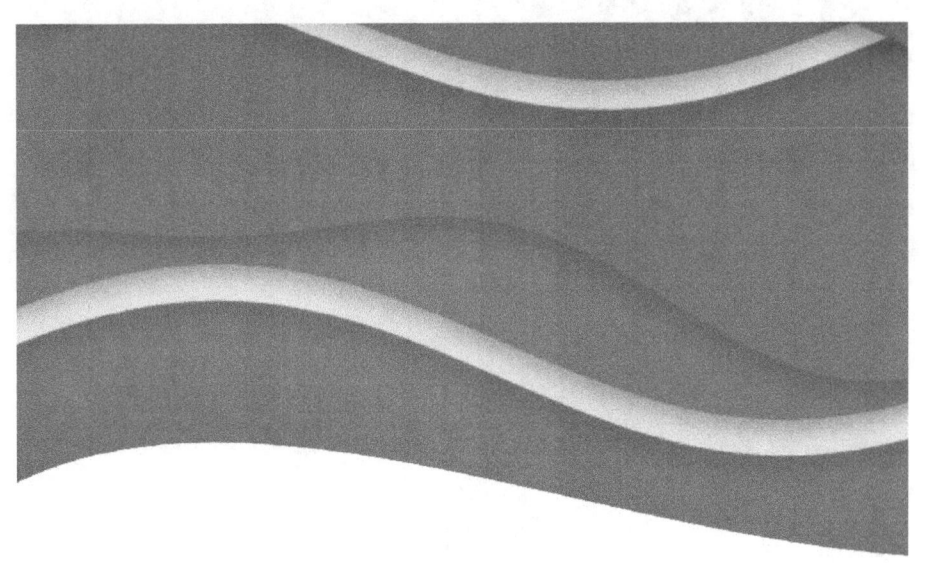

CHAPTER TWO

DISCOVERING YOUR POTENTIAL

CHAPTER
DISCOVERING YOUR POTENTIAL

> *It is necessary that we make the right choices, find out what our talents and abilities are and have them properly trained and fitted to achieve the desired end*
>
> **E. W. Kenyon**

Your potential is given to you by God. It is the gift of God in you. Also, we have established the fact that potential is a gift or talent, which has its source in God.

Everything created by God is blessed with potential. The most important principle of life is that God is a God of potential and he created everything with potential.

What you need to fulfill your dream is already in you in the form of potential as I already noted in previous chapter. Your only task is to discover it and harness it to make the best you can be. It is the responsibility of every man to discover his potential utilizes them to fulfill his purpose and dreams in life. The price to pay for success is responsibility. Until a man accepts responsibility for his life, he is not ready to fulfill destiny. The fact that you are already endowed with divine treasures cannot be overemphasized. But you have the responsibility to find out those treasures that God has put in you for the purpose of accomplishing your dreams.

Practical Ways of Discovering Potential
Prayer
Since God is the source of potential, then you need to consult Him in order to know your gifts and talents. When you pray to God and ask Him to reveal to you what He puts in you, you will receive the answer.

> Matthew 7:7-8
> *Ask, and it shall be given you; seek, and ye shall find; knock, and it shall be opened unto you:*
> *For every one that asketh receiveth; and he that seeketh findeth; and to him that knocketh it shall be opened.*

In other words, prayer is an avenue by which God

reveals your potential to you. Prayer is very important because it is our means of constantly granting God permission to interfere in the affairs of man on earth. God can do anything He wants to do, but since He has given us the freewill to operate on earth, He can release on the earth only what we allow.

Jeremiah 33:3
Call unto me, and I will answer thee, and shew thee great and mighty things, which thou knowest not.

God has promised to show you if you will ask him. When you begin to pray this way, you will begin to receive insight from heaven. When you sow a prayer, you will reap a harvest of revelation of God's deposit in you.

Martin Luther King Jr. once said; "The less I pray the harder it gets, the more I pray the better it goes."

Praying in the spirit is one major aspect of prayer that gets you in tune with divine insight. You are communication in the heavenly language and heaven will always respond with insight. When you learn the art of praying in the spirit, you are sharpening you spiritual antenna in order to hear what the spirit is saying. As you commit to it as a daily practice, you will begin to see into the great things that God has deposited in you as potential.

> *1 Corinthians 14:2*
> *For he that speaketh in an unknown tongue speaketh not unto men, but unto God: for no man understandeth him; howbeit in the spirit he speaketh mysteries.*

You need to pray daily until you begin to see those great things that God has deposited in you. God reveals your potentials to you as you ask Him in prayers.

Look Inward
Another way you can discover your potential is by looking inward into the desire of your inner man. Your inner man is always craving for physical expression. The gift in you does not want to remain dormant; it is always seeking for ways of self expression. One of your major tasks is to look inward and discover what your inner man is loaded with.

This comes by intuition most of the time. It means to know something without being told by anyone, but by the inspiration of God. You just know it by an inward witness.

Your spirit man is the inward man. It is also your heart from where all issues of life springs. That spirit man has the capacity of searching into the treasures on your inside and reveals your potential.

> Proverbs 20:27
> *The spirit of man is the candle of the LORD, searching all the inward parts of the belly.*

For instance, if you have a potential for teaching, that gift will force itself out of you as you speak to people. When you become aware of the tremendous gifts that reside within you, you are obligated to release that wealth to the world around you.

It is imperative to know that when God created you, He gave you certain gifts and talents to accomplish something He wanted. Your strongest desire, talents and opportunities reveal God's calling and potential for your life. There is no one created by God without certain endowment required to fulfill His destiny in life.

> Proverbs 18:16
> *A man's gift maketh room for him, and bringeth him before great men.*

Your gift in the form of potential will take you to great places in life when you discover and release it.

Constant and Continuous Learning

One other way to discover your full potential is to continually try to reach higher, go further, see over, and grasp something greater than you now know. And this can be done by a commitment to the study of the Word of God among other things.

The wisdom of God through the Bible is a major channel for the discovery of your potential. When you are given to the study of the book of wisdom - the Bible - you will discover what God has put in you which can change your world.

Men of great exploits and great accomplishments are

Discovering Your Potential

men who looked to the truth in the Bible and applied same to their lives. You cannot separate the gift of God in you from His Word. When you receive the truth of the Word of God, what God had deposited in you is made manifest. The scripture is the fountain of God's picture for your life. In other words, you can see a vivid picture of what stuff you are made of by looking into the scripture.

Psalm 119:18
Open thou mine eyes, that I may behold wondrous things out of thy law.

The Word of God is full of wonders that can turn you to a wonder in the world. But you need to gain the insights that are loaded in it before it can benefit you.

Also, a commitment to the reading of relevant books is another major aspect of continuous learning for discovery of your potential.

Henry Ford said; "Anyone who stops learning is old, whether at twenty or eighty. Anyone who keeps learning stays young. The greatest thing in life is to keep your mind young."

There are people who have written books related to the goals you desire to attain and they have shared the stories of how they have been able to attain theirs. All you need is to get their materials and study them to help you learn what to do to attain your own set goals in life. And as you read such materials, you will discover the abilities that God has put in you to accomplish your set goals

It is imperative, therefore, to know that there is no self-made man on earth, all men are made by what they know and such knowledge always come by constant learning from other men with result.

For instance, I discovered that God has endowed me with potential to impart knowledge to people through writing of books while reading a book many years ago. And I have committed myself to the release of that writing potential since the time I discovered it.

As you are reading this book now, you can discover your own potential. All you need is to be willing and open to divine insight packaged in it.

> Daniel 9:2
>
> *I, Daniel, was studying the writings of the prophets. I learned from the word of the LORD, as recorded by Jeremiah the prophet, that Jerusalem must lie desolate for seventy years.* (NLT)

With all the great deposit of wisdom in Daniel, he still committed himself to reading of books written by other men. No wonder he always discover more about himself from time to time.

It was Dr. Myles Munroe who said; "We are the sum total of all the individuals who have in some way, small or great, contributed to our lives. I learned everything I know from someone. We are all products of what we have gained from others."

When you engage in learning from others, you are robbing your minds with others minds from where you can discover the great deposits of God in you. Therefore, my admonition is that you read books of great men to learn what they know.

You are responsible for the discovery of your potential. And as you do, you will be determined to release and maximize it so that you will bless the world with your divine deposit. You will not add the wealth in you to the cemetery of the world. God will keep you here on earth until you die empty having released all of God's deposits in you.

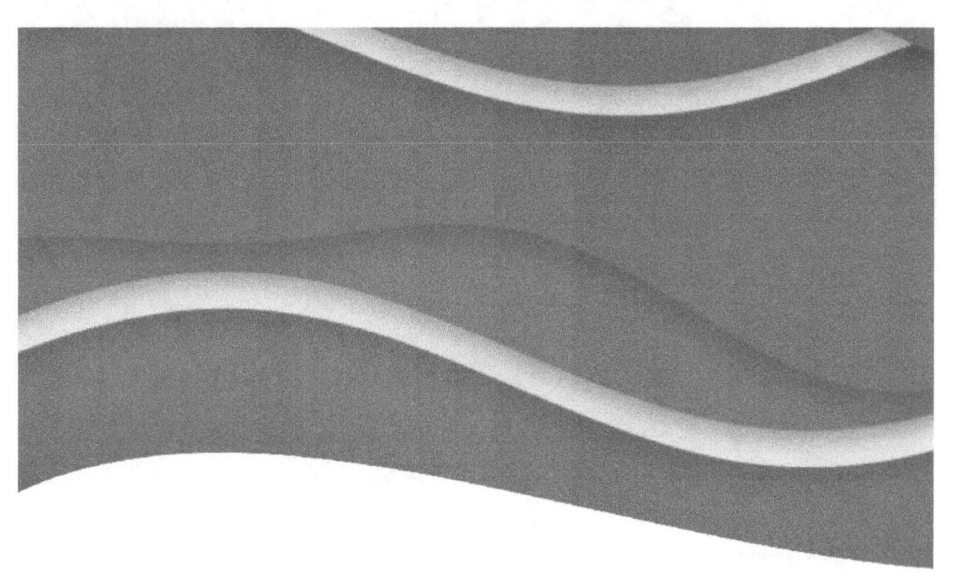

CHAPTER THREE

THE PURPOSE OF POTENTIAL

THE PURPOSE OF POTENTIAL

> *And he called ten of his slaves, and gave them ten minas and said to them, 'Do business with this until I come back.*
> **(Luke 19:13 NASU)**

The purpose of a thing is the reason why it exists. It is the motivation behind its availability. In other words, nothing exists without a reason. Just as God created all things for a purpose, He equally gave man potential for a purpose. Everything God gives is given for a purpose.

The question now is; why did God endow you with potential?

The answer to this question is this: ***potential is given to you by God for the accomplishment of the purpose for which He created you***. In other words, if you do not discover your potential and harness it properly, there is the possibility of not achieving the object of your purpose in life.

We all possess the ability to reach the top of our own unique 'Mount Everest' through a proper channeling of such divine ability in us. I have learned that true success is not so much about being talented as it is about what you do with that talent.

God has given you potential in the form of talents, gifts, ability etc; the purpose is to make you a fulfilled person in life. All the abilities, power, energy and endowment that God has put in man are all there for one thing: ***Fulfillment of Divine Purpose.***

God expects you to use the potential He gave you to carry out His assignment for you on earth. That means, you have no excuse for not fulfilling your purpose in life. This reason is that, whatever He needs to do for you He has done. All you need to do is to respond to the potential He has put in you to fulfill your purpose.

Anthony Robbins once noted; "I've continued to recognize the power individuals have to change virtually anything and everything in their lives in an instant. I've learned that the resources we need to turn our dreams into reality are within us, merely waiting for the day when we decide to wake up and claim our birthright."

The faithfulness and goodness of God is demonstrated by His commitment to His purpose for creating man. That is why He did not only show you His purpose for giving you life; He also put in you the potential required to fulfill that purpose. Therefore, He has fulfilled His part of the deal and He is awaiting your response to His Will for you on earth. Remember, your potential is what is capable of happening by your hands that are yet to happen. If you discover and unleash it, it ceases from being potential. Potential is not what you have done, rather, it is what you are capable of doing that you are yet to do. Before you accomplish any task in the pursuit of your purpose, that thing was potential, but by the time the task is accomplished, it is no longer potential.

God gave you potential because, He did not only want you to carry out your purpose, but to finish the assignment He gave you on earth. Your glory is hidden in the completion of your assignment and you can only complete your assignment in life by discovering and utilizing the potential that God put in you. You are only termed successful when you finish you assignment.

Again, Dr. Myles Munroe said; "The wealthiest spot on earth is not the oil field of Iraq, neither is it the gold mines of the world, but it is the cemetery."

In the cemeteries of the world are buried potential in the form of dreams that never saw the light of day, businesses that were never started, paintings that were never painted, ministries that were never began, books that were never written and inventions that were never invented. All these unreleased potential are given by God for fulfilling purpose, but once a man dies, he died with the potential. The death of an unfulfilled man is the death of potential and it equals to increase in the wealth buried in the cemetery.

Only God can tell of how much wealthy the

cemeteries of the world are. And only He has the accurate statistical data of the wealth being added to the ones already in the cemeteries on a daily basis. This is as a result of people dying with their God-given endowment in the form of potential. God is not happy with men who are not fulfilled. Therefore, you must make up your mind to discover your purpose and potential and release them for your fulfillment in life so that they will not be added to the wealth in the cemetery.

God has designed that you will fulfill your life's purpose by accomplishing different tasks involved one after the other, phase by phase and precept upon precept. The ones you have accomplished are no longer potential, the next task to be accomplished is your potential, because potential is what can happen through you that are yet to happen.

God is always looking forward to what is next after one task is accomplished. He is always interested in the release of the potential He has put in you. The greatest enemy of progress is success. And success is the greatest enemy of success. This is because; most times people get carried away by the celebration of the last success and never move to the next level of success. Therefore, they have allowed today's success which is a product of released potential, to blind them to the remaining potential in them which will bring the next level of success and fulfillment of divine purpose.

Do not allow what you have accomplished today become a blockage to what more you could accomplish. You will always need to accomplish certain task in order to fulfill your purpose as I earlier noted. Many people in life have accomplished some very great and outstanding feats and they stop at that while God is expecting the potential for greater things remaining in them to be unleashed.

Why must you 'rest on your oars' when you are capable of getting more and greater results? Why must you allow your last success to eternally impede the next level of success that is still in you as your potential? Why do you think that the cemetery is worthy of the great potential that God has put in you for greater level of accomplishment?

The Purpose Of Potential

Until you release all the potential in you, you have not fulfilled your purpose, because God gave you potential to fulfill His purpose for you. God's thoughts about you are good and He expects His best in you to be released as a blessing to the world. Your death will only be precious to Him at end of your time on earth, if you finish your course (purpose) by releasing all the potential in you.

> Psalm 116:15
>
> *Precious in the sight of the LORD is the death of his saints.*

God does not take pleasure in the death of anyone who died with the potential He has put in them, even if they lived for 500 years. You must release all the potential that God has put in you in order to fulfill your purpose before your time on earth is over. And the earlier you understand this truth the better for you as one ordained as a blessing to the world.

You must understand that the valuable potential that God puts in you in not just for your own benefit, but for enriching the lives of others. It is your personal responsibility to discover and utilize it for the purpose of accomplishing your mandate on earth.

Divine Purpose and Potential

Basil Walsh said; "We don't need more strength or more ability or greater opportunity. What we need to use is what we have."

You are capable of getting more results than what you presently have. And as a matter of fact, the fulfillment of your purpose will happen phase by phase. You will move from one level of glory to another level until you will reach the time that the whole earth will be filled with the glory of your fulfilled purpose as the water covers the sea.

What is Purpose?

It is important to know that your purpose is the end goal that drives your current actions. It is the reason that you work on the things you do and the outcome you wish to achieve by your efforts. God is a God of purpose. He created all things for a purpose and the ignorance of purpose results in lack of fulfillment of destiny.

The Purpose Of Potential

Purpose is God's original intention for creating man. It is the reason why God made man. Also, purpose is God's motivation for manufacturing man. It is God-ordained destination for man. It also means God's determination and resolution about man, His product. It is the 'why' of God for man on earth. Purpose is God's intended result for which He created man. And it is God's established end for which man was started.

No man exists on earth without a peculiar intention in God's mind before the creation. It is what God had in mind as His purpose for man that necessitated his being created. In other word, every man on earth came because there is a purpose God intended him to fulfill. If that purpose was not there, creation would not have occurred. God has a peculiar purpose for every man and whether that purpose is fulfilled or not depends on man's decision to understand, discover and pursue that purpose of God for creating him.

Michel de Montaigne once noted; "The soul which has no fixed purpose in life is lost; to be everywhere, is to be nowhere".

It is God's purpose for man that determine His priority, motivation and commitment to man. No manufacturer will ever go into production without first establishing what purpose his product will perform. And in the same way, God created man according to the purpose He had in mind for him before the foundation of the world. Your life's purpose is the original intent or predetermined result of God for you; it is God's expected end for you. The only true source of definition for anything in life is the original purpose for its existence. When you have discovered yourself and your unique purpose and identity, only then can you fully contribute to the lives of others.

There is the need to understand that your purpose in life is not what you want to do; neither is it what you think you should do, rather, it is what God has created you to do. It is what God intended for you before He created you. And you are not to determine that; only God who created you knows the purpose for which He has created you. All you need is to find out from Him. This is because until you know what you are created to do, you may not know what to pursue in life.

Success in life is the fulfillment of the original intent or purpose established by the manufacturer of a product or the initiator and source of an assignment. You cannot measure your success by comparing what you have done in life with what others have done; rather, your success is measured by comparing what you have done with what you are created to do. In God's perspective, a man is a success when he has fulfilled divine purpose, no matter what other things he might have done. Even if he has achieved many things in life, as long as those things are not consistent with his God-given purpose, he is not a success

However, understand that, it is your responsibility to discover that definite purpose of God for creating you which will make you a success in the race of life. Just as I earlier noted, the key of advancement in the school of destiny is the discovery, understanding and unleashing of your purpose and potential.

Your purpose is your God-given life assignment and it is just one thing that you are born to do, but God has given you potential to aid in fulfilling that one purpose. You must note that purpose cannot be fulfilled without potential as they are needed to carry out certain tasks within the context of your purpose. Potential helps in actualizing the reality of your purpose. God created you for one thing – ***purpose***, but He endowed you with many divine abilities – ***potential***. Therefore, purpose and potential are inseparable in our bid to fulfill destiny. You came into this world pregnant with unlimited potential which God put in you to fulfill you purpose on earth.

Norman Vincent Paele said; "Anybody can do just about anything with himself that he really wants to and makes up his mind to do. We are capable of greater things than we realize."

Just as every manufacturer puts in his product all the abilities required for the product to fulfill its one-established purpose, in the same way, God has put in man, His product, all the abilities required to fulfill the one-established purpose for him. God cannot demand from His products what He did not supply to it. God cannot ask a lion to roar if He has not put the ability to roar in it. He cannot demand fish to swim if He did not put that ability in it, and he will not demand a bird to fly if the potential to fly is not inherent in it. Consequently, God cannot demand from man what He did not supply to man. God created man for a purpose and He put in man all the abilities required by man to carry out the purpose to fulfillment.

For instance, God will not call a man to preach if He has not put in him the ability to preach. He will not demand songs from man that He did not supply with singing ability. Whatever God has ordained you to do in life; He has equally supplied you with the potential to accomplish that purpose. But it is your responsibility to discover that purpose and the inherent ability that will enable you fulfill the purpose.

It is your season of exploits as you accept responsibility for your destiny.

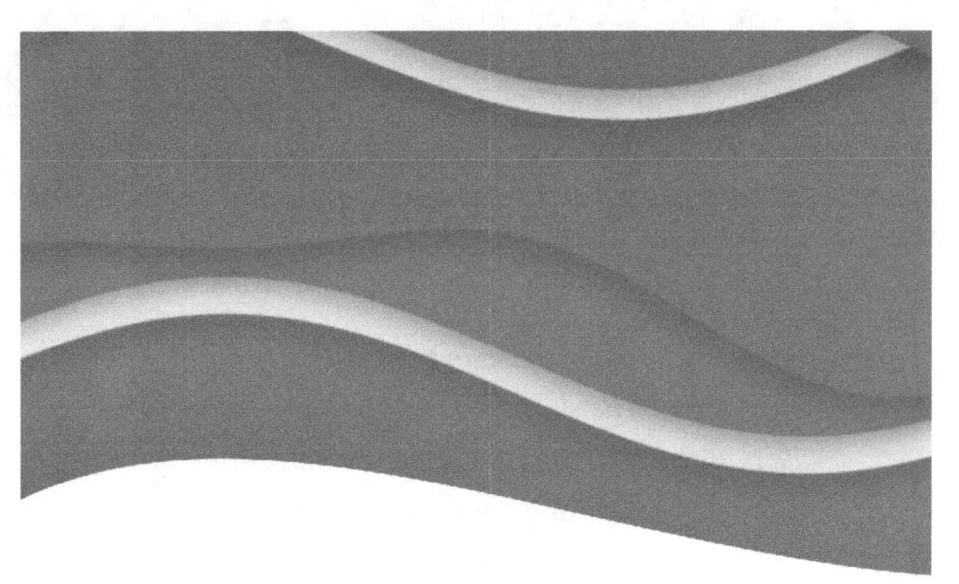

CHAPTER
FOUR

RELEASING YOUR POTENTIAL

RELEASING YOUR POTENTIAL

Man has been programmed by God to do only according to what he knows. But he has been given the ability to program himself to do more daily by knowing more daily as he learns more daily
Sunday A. Ezekiel

Potential unreleased equals destiny unaccomplished, purpose not fulfilled and vision truncated. The tragedy of life is that potential in a man is not transferable to another. The man given potential is the one to release it or otherwise, his death automatically results in the death of such potential.

That is why I established earlier on that the grave yards (cemeteries) of the world are loaded with the greatest wealth that was denied of the world. Quite a lot of great businesses, inventions, dreams et cetera such that would have created great financial and material wealth for the world have been buried in the grave yards of the world. Why? The carrier of such great potential died with them.

How I wish it were possible to transfer one's potential to another person, some of the great stuff that died with the carriers would have been transferred to other before they died.

For instance, what do you think would have happened in the world if great potential such as the invention of automobile, computer, telephone, airplane, electricity, incandescent light bulb, et cetera had died with the inventors?

Perhaps we would have still remained in the Stone Age which is characterized with the use of stone to make tools and weapons. The truth is that many things would remain impossible to accomplish without these inventions.

We will forever be grateful to God for the birth of great people like Henry Ford, Alexander Graham Bell, The Wright brothers, Michael Faraday, Thomas Edison et cetera. But note that we are celebrating them because they released their God-given potential to transform our world and they chose not to add these great inventions to the wealth in the grave yards of the world. However, I believe that there are a lot of people like them who died full of what would have benefited our world today. They went to the grave yard unfulfilled, unaccomplished and unreleased.

You must make up your mind that the wealth in grave yard of the world is enough to have your own potential added to it. You must decide never to allow your inventions, businesses, dreams, vision trapped in you to die with you. You need to awake the giant that God has deposited in you and release it to bless mankind.

The death of a seed equals to the burial and funeral of a forest. That seed in you must not die or else, the world will be robbed of the forests of blessings inherent in it. There is something that the world has never seen or known that you are loaded with. You must release it to bless the world. It is in you, arise to discover it a release it. You are the next wonder that the world has been waiting for. I am eager to read about your released potential in the form of your discovered purpose, dreams and vision becoming a reality. I am waiting to read your book and to benefit from your great inventions.

> Romans 8:19
>
> *For the earnest expectation of the creature waiteth for the manifestation of the sons of God.*

However, the starting point in releasing your potential is to first understand and discover it. You cannot release what you are not aware of. You need to know the abilities that are loaded in you and we have established that truth in the previous chapters.

Also, it is the knowledge of purpose that gives a clue to the potential loaded in a product. When you do not know what a product is made for, you may not know what it can do. Therefore, the knowledge of potential comes from the knowledge of purpose. And the releasing of your potential is not up to God but you, because it is your responsibility.

When you purchase a product from the store, there must be a purpose for which that product was manufactured. Also, you must have purchased it in order to fulfill the purpose for which the manufacturer stated in the manual to meet your need. However, you may not be aware of what it can do if you are not aware of why it was made.

In the same way, if you do not know why you are made, you will be ignorant of what you can do. There is no way you will be able to release your potential until you have discovered your purpose. Once you lay hold on your God given purpose, your potential will begin to show up gradually.

A Commitment To Productive Work

The release of your potential is done by commitment to productive work involved in the task of your purpose. Nothing works until it is worked.

Proverbs 22:29

*Seest thou a man **diligent in his business**? he shall stand before kings; he shall not stand before mean men.*

Your purpose is your God-given life business. And as you commit yourself to doing that business in pursuit of your purpose, you are releasing your potential. Therefore, potential is released through productive engagement in tasks line with your discovered purpose.

For instance, if your discovered purpose is teaching business, your daily commitment to leaning and teaching is the release of your potential which leads to the fulfillment of that purpose.

Also, if your own discovered purpose is preaching of the gospel, your potential will be released as you engage in working productively everyday on soul winning, church planting, preaching and such other activities depending on your specific area of calling.

If your own discovered purpose is creative invention and innovation, you will release your potential as you work productively on inventing products/services or innovating business solutions that will solve people's problems.

Whatever is your discovered purpose, your potential

which came with your purpose will be released as you commit to productive work. It is important to note that race horses do not win race while they are still in the stall; rather, they must participate in the race by getting to the field.

> 1 Corinthians 15:10
>
> *But by the grace (the unmerited favor and blessing) of God I am what I am, and His grace toward me was not [found to be] for nothing (fruitless and without effect). In fact, **I worked harder than all of them** [the apostles], though it was not really I, but the grace (the unmerited favor and blessing) of God which was with me.* (AMP)

That means, as you work out what is in you; you are releasing your potential. You need to build your daily agenda around your discovered purpose, because, it is your life business. Each task you perform everyday, is a release of your potential. Therefore, without work, you cannot release your potential and you cannot fulfill your purpose without releasing your potential. It is through work that your potential is released to bless the world.

It takes diligence, which is hard work in the right direction to release your potential. That potential can die with you if you do not release it. You have a responsibility for the release of your potential to fulfill your destiny. It takes work to achieve greatness. No one talks about greatness without work. It is through work that people become who they are; because God gives you work to activate your power. Work is simply the activation of possibilities.

There in the need to understand that work is not the same as a job. It is not a job that releases potential, it is work. Job only provides you a pay cheque at the end of the month. You can be on a job and not be committed to work. Many people hold on to a job because of security, not that they are actually working. There is nothing as depressing and frustrating than having someone on a job who is not interested in working. Work is God's pathway to a meaningful and effective living. When you refuse to work, you deny yourself the opportunity to fulfill your purpose. You are not born a genius; rather you can become one by working to release what you have. Work is the key to your personal progress, productivity and fulfillment of destiny.

Farrah Gray said; "Job means 'Just over Broke' that is, one pay cheque away from being evicted."

Work is God's way of revealing your talents, abilities and capabilities. When you have a dream, then it is time to work out its fulfillment and that requires the use of your potential, but that potential is released by hard work. Work arises from the desire to contribute to the world's wealth and well-being by giving of what you have been given by God in the form of potential.

It is only through work that you can do and become all that God originally intended for your life. God does not give potential for fun; He expects it to be released as you work it out through committed, smart and creative work. Potential without work remains untapped. It remains unused and untested.

Another way to define work is the use of your God-given abilities and faculties to do or perform a task. Your purpose in life is a task, but you have been given potential to achieve it. It is as you commit yourself to work that the potential is released to accomplish the task. You need to release your potential to accomplish your purpose or it remains unaccomplished.

Do not go to the grave yard with that dream of yours, it has great possibilities but you must work out your potential to fulfill it. Your success is not determined by what you have, but by what you do with what you have.

Until you start working out your potential, you do not stand to benefit the world with the power that you are endowed with. Work is part of God's design for you. You are created to work. Your refusal to work is not revealing the image of God that you are. If you do not work that potential, it remains dormant and useless. And God will not be happy about it.

Janice Krouskop once noted; "Without ambition one starts nothing, and without hard work one finishes nothing. Therefore, those who stretch their backbone to reach their wish bone will make things happen".

It is only in the dictionary that you will see that

success comes before work. But in real life, it is work before success. Work must come first before success can be achieved. Successful accomplishment of a dream is a direct product of hard work.

In his poem, William Pedrin wrote; "No pain, no palm, No cross, no crown, No thorn, no throne, No gall, no glory!"

Work is a must in order to release your potential. You cannot really know how much you can achieve until you put your hands to work. You are capable of doing more than you have done, but that can only be known through your commitment to work.

That gift in you is called potential, that talent in you is called potential. That divine endowment is called potential. But it is given to you for your accomplishment and it is your personal responsibility to understand, discover and release it. As you do so, you cannot but accomplish your God-given purpose in life.

Understand that the best preparation for good work tomorrow is to do good work today, because the good work of today is to discover your potential and release it to fulfill your destiny so that tomorrow, you will generate great impact in your own generation.

A wise man once said; "Some dream of worthy accomplishments while others stay awake and do them."

You must stay awake and work hard, work smart and work fast to release your potential and accomplish your dream in life.

Work has great benefits among which are:

Work brings divine privilege to fulfill destiny.
It is by working that you become the person that God has ordained you to become. When you locate your purpose and begin to work towards it fulfillment, you are utilizing of your God-given potential to realize your dream.

Work brings increase and multiplication
When you are committed to working on your ideas and dreams according to your discovered purpose, you will increase and your wealth will multiply in the

process. Poverty is a result of laziness while wealth and prosperity are products of hard work.

Work is a release of your faith
Without work, that is, consistent action on your dream, you are only revealing your lack of faith in your dream. As you work daily on your discovered purpose and dream, you are acting your faith that will ensure its fulfillment.

Work makes you a blessing
As you keep working on your purpose, you are releasing your potential which is given to you for the fulfillment of that purpose. Your released potential through work brings you to the fulfillment of that purpose and you automatically become a blessing to mankind.

It is your season of impact and exploits, but you must accept personal responsibility to release your potential through a commitment to hard, smart and creative work.

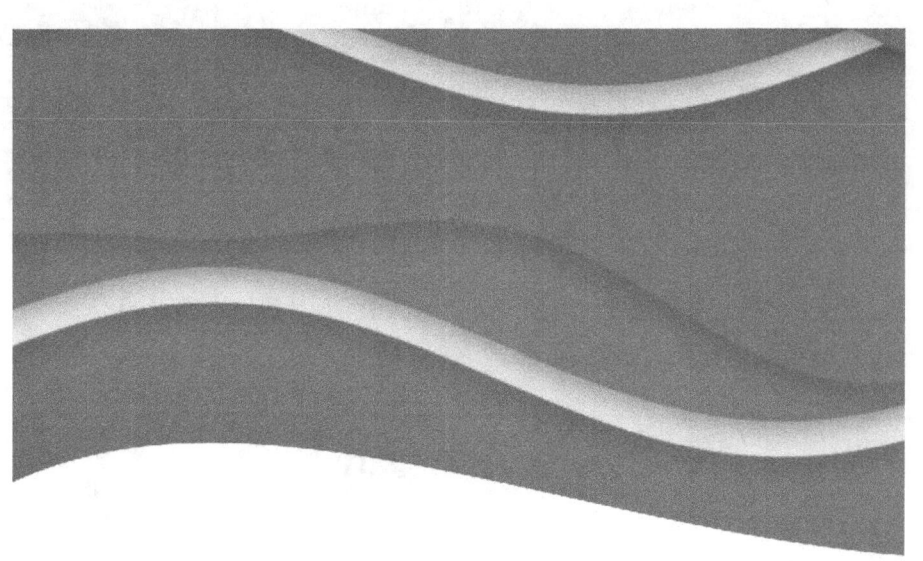

CHAPTER
FIVE

MAXIMIZING YOUR POTENTIAL

CHAPTER
MAXIMIZING YOUR POTENTIAL

So he shepherded them according to the integrity of his heart, And guided them by the skillfulness of his hands.

(Psalm 78:72 NKJV)

There are hundreds of thousands or millions of people born or yet to be born who are to benefit from your unreleased potential. They are ordained to read that book you are yet to write. The are ordained to benefit from that business you are yet to start, that song you are yet to compose or that ministry you are yet to begin.

God expects the great treasure in you in form of potential to be maximized and released to benefit mankind. Just as many have released their treasure to bless you, your own treasure must be released to bless others. The Manufacturer of man designed everything not only to reproduce itself but also to transfer and transmit its life and treasure in form of potential to the next generation.

However, your potential can be maximized in order to generate greater result than you are presently having. You are ordained by God for global impact. In other words, your results are ordained to affect the entire world positively. And that can only become real as you maximize your potential.

The question now is: **How do I Maximize My Potential?**

Your skillfulness determines your level of result. When your skill level increases, you are bound to generate greater result than you presently have. In other words, the more skilful you become, the more impactful your result. It is skillfulness that leads to competence and competence in delivering your task maximizes your potential.

The productive performance level of a worker to meet set goals and objective is determined by skillfulness and competence. These are equally of great importance in the full release of potential and fulfillment of God's purpose for man. They help you to accomplish your task faster and better than you would have done without them. This is because; your potential can be enhanced for its full release when you possess the right and necessary skill and competence.

Training is the key to increased skill level and competence. In other words, personal and specialized trainings are the keys to maximizing man's potential.

Someone had said; "The pursuit of education is predicated on the acceptance that a degree of ignorance already exists. You cannot be taught things that you already know — you can only be reminded that you already knew them. 'I can't be expected to know everything.' That's very true — but you are expected to learn all that you possibly can about your own life, as a failure to do so will have serious repercussions for you".

There is the need to be subjected to the required personal and specialized training relevant to your discovered purpose in order to acquire the necessary skill and competence that will maximize your potential for its full release. This will lead to great and impactful result in your accomplishments.

Training can be defined as the act of learning specified skill by practice. Also, it means, the process of attaining physical efficiency by exercise. Training is a major virtue for learning, because, it enables you to achieve effectiveness in your assignment.

I am sure you have discovered your God-given purpose in life. You need to move to the level of discovering and releasing your potential as you engage in the required training for the acquisition of the necessary skill and competence. This will help you maximize your potential for maximum productivity and impact in the fulfillment of your destiny.

Your potential is given you to bless the world, not to be added to the wealth in the cemetery. You are expected to die empty of potential at the end of your life on earth having fulfilled you purpose. Remember, when a seed dies, a forest is buried, because, the seed carries the potential of a forest. Within a seed is trapped a tree which has fruit that has seed and the seed has trees that has fruit which has seeds that bring forth a forest of trees.

God does not desire any man dies as a seed; rather, He wants the forest of great trees trapped in us to be released to bless the world. This is a very deep mystery that you need to pay full attention to in order to fulfill your destiny as ordained by God.

You are about to be released to your world as you release your potential. Impact begins with a discovery of purpose, but it is the release and maximizing of your potential that leads to the fulfillment of that discovered purpose.

CHAPTER
SIX

BEWARE OF POTENTIAL LIMITING FORCES

CHAPTER
BEWARE OF POTENTIAL LIMITING FORCES

> *The nature of the composition of the source materials determines the nature of the composition of the product made or produced from it.*
>
> **Dr. Myles Munroe**

Your potential is determined by the potential of God who is the Source from where you came. In other words, what you carry is what God carries because; he poured Himself into you at creation.

> Genesis 1:26
>
> *Let us make man in our image, after our likeness: and let them have dominion over the fish of the sea, and over the fowl of the air, and over the cattle, and over all the earth, and over every creeping thing that creepeth upon the earth.*

However, there are certain forces that can hinder that great divine deposit in the form of potential from being fully released. It will discuss some of these factors in this chapter. When you identify them, you will be able to deal with them so as not to be hindered from becoming a blessing that God has made you to your world.

Sin

Sin is the result of disobedience to the known will of God. You are created in God's image and likeness. That means you have in you what God has in Him. In other words, your potential is determined by God's potential and your ability is determined by His ability.

However, the release of that potential will be hindered by disobedience to God's will for your life. The reason is that, when you sin, the force in you that makes you "God-like" is limited from manifest. Death is the penalty for sin. The God force in man dies when he sins. And when that happens, the potential in him dies too.

> Ezekiel 18:4
> *Behold, all souls are mine; as the soul of the father,*

> *so also the soul of the son is mine:* **the soul that sinneth, it shall die.**

There has to be a reconnection back to God through Jesus Christ before man can fully release his God-given potential.

In addition, there are many things in life that are not necessarily wrong in themselves, but they will hinder the full release of your potential. These could be things that hinder you from growing spiritually to match up with God's program in following His purpose for your life. It is important to identify and lay them aside so that you can release your potential and fulfill your purpose in life.

Self-Serving Attitude

Kate Halverson said; "If you are all wrapped up in yourself, you are over dressed."

Self-serving attitude means, thinking only of self, tending to concentrate selfishly on your own needs and affairs and to show little or no interest in those of others.

This attitude limits man's potential. The reason is that your potential is not given to your for self gratification. Rather, it is given you for the benefit of other people. Every great and big dream is people-focused and others-centered. Small thinking focuses on self, while big thinking focuses on others. There is no way a selfish attitude can obtain divine help from God for full release of potential.

In addition, when you are self-focused, you will not learn from others. And if you do not learn from others, your view about life will be very limited; hence your potential for greatness will not be fully released. Also, real and effective leadership springs from a heart willing and ready to serve others. A leader does not boss over people; rather, he serves people by influencing them to fulfill their God-given purpose and dream on earth. His leadership potential will not be released if he is self-serving.

This attitude must be dealt with if you really desire to be a blessing to the world. Start focusing on how you can be of help to people around you and you will begin to release the great treasure in the form of potential that God has put in you.

Beware Of Potential Limiting Forces

You are born to serve and when you serve, you become a leader that God has made you to be.

Fear

The fear of failure is a limiting factor for potential. You must refuse to fear if you desire to release your potential and fulfill your purpose. Fear will cripple you from making certain moves that you need to make and it will hinder you from taking the risks involve in your pursuit without which fulfillment will not be in view. Do not be afraid to fail. The truth is, you will never succeed greatly until you are willing to fail greatly. As a matter of fact, it is better to have tried and failed than to not have tried and never know you could have succeeded.

> 2 Timothy 1:7
> *For God hath not given us the spirit of fear; but of power, and of love, and of a sound mind.*

God has not given you the spirit of fear. In other words, fear is a spirit from the devil. Therefore you must fight against it so that it will not limit your potential in life. You must be bold to confront the spirit of fear and deal with is through the Spirit of God. That way you will be able to fully release your potential and become a blessing to your world.

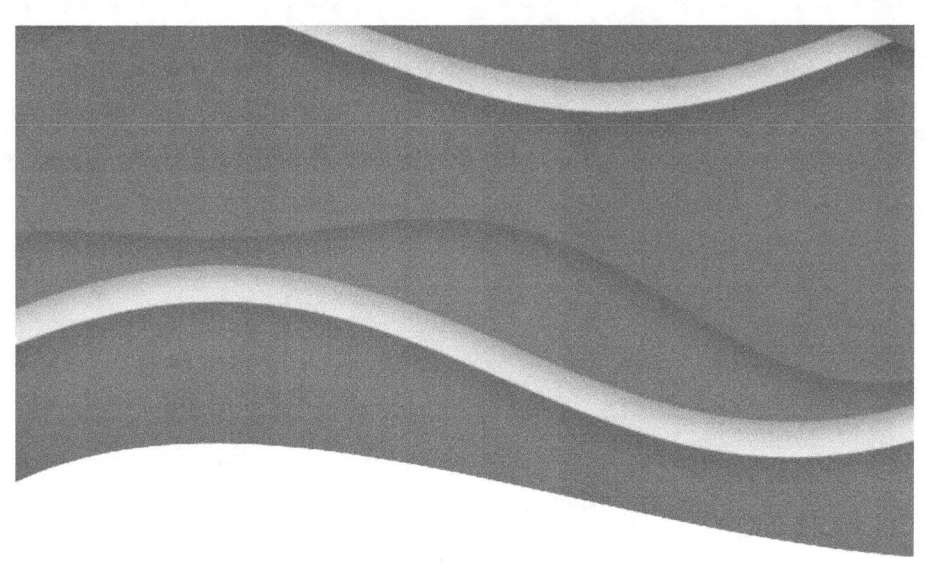

CHAPTER
SEVEN

KEEP PRESSING ON!

KEEP PRESSING ON!

> *Brethren, I count not myself to have apprehended: but this one thing I do, forgetting those things which are behind, and reaching forth unto those things which are before,* **I press toward the mark** *for the prize of the high calling of God in Christ Jesus.*
> **(Philippians 3:13-14)**

It is only those who will keep moving in the pursuit of destiny that will emerge in greatness in this season of impact. Those who give up too soon never realize how close they were to the reality of their destiny.

You need to keep releasing what is on your inside until you are left with nothing. Remember, potential once released ceases from being potential. There is more trapped in you to be released.

You have been given all you will ever need to fulfill your purpose. The potential to carry out all the tasks involved in your assignment in life are inherent in you. But it is your responsibility to keep releasing them from time to time until you reach the top of your own unique 'Mount Everest'.

You need to understand that great works are performed by perseverance, persistence and patience and only few things are impossible to diligence and skillfulness.

It was Will Rogers who said; "Even if you are on the right track, you will get run over if you just sit there."

Do not be satisfied with your present level of result and become complacent about life; there are yet great things loaded in you that must not go the grave with you. You must decide today to release all those treasures. Stop wishing and start willing. Stop proposing and start purposing. Stop procrastinating and start planning. Be determined not to add your 'stuffs' to the cemetery. Choose not to deny the world of the great treasures trapped in you. No matter how slow your pace may appear, keep at it.

Martin Luther King Jr. said; "If you cannot fly, run. If

you cannot run, walk. If you cannot walk, crawl. By all means keep moving! I have kept moving."

You need to see beyond your loins and start moving into the future. Only those who chose to see beyond their present actually become world changers. It may not be convenient now, but remember that great works are not accomplished on the platter of gold; neither is great accomplishment deliver with convenience. Refuse to settle for the average and move on to excellence in your result.

The fact that you are still living is evidence that you posses something that can benefit the world, no matter what you have achieve before now.

Put Your Faith To Work

Hebrews 11:6
But without faith it is impossible to please him: for he that cometh to God must believe that he is, and that he is a rewarder of them that diligently seek him.

Every outstanding result is a product of faith in

action and the release of you potential is a release of your faith. That means in the absence of faith nothing tangible can happen in life. Faith is what God expects from us for Him to accomplish anything in our lives.

Someone once said; "God has tied Himself irrevocably to human cooperation in the execution of divine purposes. He has made man's faith a determining factor in the work of redemption."

It suffices to admit that, until your faith is in place, God remains 'helpless' in your case. Also, faith is the confident assurance that what you have discovered about yourself in God is real even though you cannot see it physically yet. Faith begins by hearing a certain sound that other people cannot hear. Our hearing has a lot to do with our having. No man has ever fulfilled any divine mandate on this earth without operating active faith for the reality of that mandate. And you faith in the truth that God's ability is what determines your ability is what will trigger the full release of your potential to fulfill your destiny.

If you do not believe in the possibility of your destiny, it is as good as not having discovered it in the first place. Your faith in the possibility of your destiny is what will cause a drive in your inner man to advance against all adversities towards its fulfillment. Your pursuit in life is simply a direct revelation of what you believe. Faith is the greatest miracle working power in the world. No man can fail with faith.

However, faith for discovering, releasing and maximizing your potential will come to you as you keep learning at the feet of Jesus who is the Source of your potential. The more of His Word you read, hear, study, memorize and meditate upon, the more faith you posses in His divine ability in you.

> Romans 10:17
> *So then faith cometh by hearing, and hearing by the word of God.*

You must believe in yourself and have faith in your God-given abilities. Without a humble but reasonable confidence in your own God-given powers you cannot be successful.

It is important to believe in the fact that God has deposited great potential in you that will enhance the fulfillment of your destiny, because he made you in His very image. In addition, your understanding of the truth that the life of God is in you will help you to believe in your God-given ability. Also, it will help you a lot in the way you treat yourself which will determine the way others will treat you.

As I earlier noted, what you can accomplish in life is dependent on what God has created you to do. Whatever you are created to do you can successfully accomplish because His strength is available to carry out His task for you. Your faith is foolproof assurance, God's confirmation, the title deed guaranteeing that the change you want will take place if you act on it.

One thing that kills the potential miracle working power of faith is lack of self- confidence. That means if you do not believe in the great things that God can make happen through you, you cannot fully release you potential to accomplish you purpose in life. The best way to get to this level of faith is by appreciating every good thing that God has put in you.

> **Philemon 6**
> *That the communication of thy faith may become effectual by the acknowledging of every good thing which is in you in Christ Jesus.*

You are loaded with divine treasure in the form of potential and that is all you need to fulfill your destiny. But you must understand it, discover it, and release it for maximum accomplishment in life.

The world is waiting to partake of the blessings of your potential. That great dream in you must see the light of day. That great business empire in you must be released to bless the world. That powerful book must be written to bless the world. And that great invention must come to life as a solution to the world's problem. You are a blessing to your generation and the next. Choose to respond to what God has put in you and you will become the next celebrity.

It is your turn to become the best you can be as you discover, develop, release and maximize your potential.

GET CONNECTED

In case you have read this book and you are yet to receive Jesus as your personal Lord and Savior, please, say these words as your act of submission to God's redemption plan:

Thank you Heavenly Father for sending Your Son Jesus to save me. Lord Jesus, I believe that you died and resurrected to save me, I ask that you come into my life today. Forgive me of my sin, cleanse me with your blood and accept me in the beloved. I confess you as my Lord and Savior today. Now I know that I am born again and saved from sin and the world. Thank you Lord for saving me. Amen.

I congratulate you for making this great decision today and I pray that you will not fall apart in your walk with God in this new-found faith in Christ.

If this book has been of great blessing to you, please write us through our emails or send SMS or give us a call through our phones numbers to share your testimonies. You can also connect with us through our Facebook pages and website.

Do not fail to recommend this book to other people as a way of being a blessing to them in contributing to the fulfillment of their God-ordained purposes in life.

In addition, we welcome your comments and views about the book so as to know how we can serve you and other people in a better way.

Thank you. We love you

Pastor Sunday A. Ezekiel being commissioned to the ministry by his spiritual father, Bishop David O. Oyedepo on the 20th of April 2012

Pastor Sunday A. Ezekiel with Rev. Sam Adeyemi, 2015 and 2017

Become The Best! Release Your Potential

Other Books By The Same Author

1. Become The Best! Release Your Potential
2. Dream Big and Succeed
3. Living Your Vision
4. Purpose Power Secrets
5. Your Dream Creates Your Future

ABOUT THE AUTHOR

Sunday Adeniyi Ezekiel is an ordained Pastor, Insightful Teacher, Creative and Innovative Leadership Coach, with a visionary mandate to raise a people of impact and Exploits.

Ordained into an independent ministry by Bishop David Oyedepo of Living Faith Church a.k.a. Winners Chapel International after serving as a Pastor for some years in the headquarters in Canaan Land.

He is the President and Senior Pastor of DREAMERS WORLD CHRISTIAN CENTRE (a.k.a Faith Impact Chapel Int'l) Lagos, Nigeria.

As an astute business magnate with a passion to help people create lasting wealth, he is the co-founder, Executive Director and member of the Board of Directors of RICHLIFE COMMERCIAL AND LOGISTICTS LIMITED, a fast growing real estate company with two major brands namely RICHLIFE ESTATE AND GARDENS and RICHLIFE ROYAL CITY with over 500 network of Associates spread across Lagos, other parts of Nigeria and abroad.

He holds a Diploma in Public Accounting and Auditing from Kwara State Polytechnic, Ilorin and BSc in Business Administration from Lagos State University.
He is also a graduate of Leadership Diploma from Word of Faith Bible Institute (WOFBI) and Leadership Certificate from Daystar Leadership Academy (DLA), Lagos.

He is happily married to his lovely wife Helen who is a co-labourer in the work of the ministry. They are blessed with children; Oyindamola, Olamiposi and Olasurubomi.

www.ingramcontent.com/pod-product-compliance
Lightning Source LLC
Chambersburg PA
CBHW070206230526
45471CB00002B/837